THIERRY ROLLET

Léo Ferré. Artist of Life

First published by Editions Dedicaces in 2018

Copyright © Thierry Rollet, 2018

All rights reserved. No part of this publication may be reproduced, stored or transmitted in any form or by any means, electronic, mechanical, photocopying, recording, scanning, or otherwise without written permission from the publisher. It is illegal to copy this book, post it to a website, or distribute it by any other means without permission.

First edition

ISBN: 9781770767348

Translation by Caroline Andreea Zgortea

This book was professionally typeset on Reedsy. Find out more at reedsy.com

*"Our language, to us other artists,
is within reach of all ears
and of all eyes,
because it is songs, light, shapes, smiles."*

Léo Ferré, The bad Seed

Contents

Foreword   iii

I   "SONG" or Léo Ferré, a man who sings

My Way of 5 Songs	3
Who Are You, Ferré?	7
The Beginning of a Child of the Entertainment	10
From Odéon to Barclay	15

II   "LIGHT" or Ferré, a man who grows

A Composer before Anything Else	21
The Poet, The Poets	25
The Singer, The Singers	31
With Time...	34

III   "GALBE" / "CONTOUR" or Ferré, a man who indisposes

Love-Anarchy	39
The Producer	46
Léo-Benoît, Ferré-Misère	49
Memory and the Sea	53

IV   "SMILE" or Ferré, a man who lives

The Artist and his Public	59
A Genius of Parody	62

In a Madness of Colors and Sounds	64
Ferré 2008	67
Excerpts of Fundamental Texts	69
Bibliography	72
Favorite Discography	74
Interesting Websites	76
Notes	77
About the Author	80

Foreword

The 15th anniversary of Léo Ferré's death marks the rediscovery of one of the greatest personalities of French song and poetry.

At least, this is what the general public will easily understand. The aficionados, and most of all, Léo's "heirs" will surely know that it's about rediscovering a true apostle of music.

Ferré was a musician at heart, especially as he also sang. But it is music that made his work multifaceted, be it poetic or literary.

PART I

"SONG" or Léo Ferré, a man who sings

One

My Way of 5 Songs

OR me, Léo Ferré, was *a man who sang* – otherwise said, not what I would call a *singer*, in the time when I was between 13 and 20 years old.

Léo Ferré, was *Pretty kid, Paris blackguard, With time, The Poets, C'est extra*, songs I knew and I could listen to on RTL or Europe 1 – the "free radios", the FM bandwidth not being popularized yet – without feeling the irresistible urge to change stations or cut the sound; this is the reason why I was saying I *could* listen to them. Brassens, Brel, Béart, Ferrat, Gainsbourg, Leclerc, Mouloudji, Moustaki, was the group of which Ferré was a part of: that of *men who sing*, not *singers*.

I can imagine I'm starting to raise a lot of eyebrows, not to mention shoulders. So I'll try to clarify, to explain my goal.

These men who were singing were «committed singers»: this is the term with which I became acquainted at 16 years of age, thanks to the kindness of some school colleagues, who charitably instructed me in regards to the subject of this honorable singers' caste. Before, I was totally ignorant. For me, singers were those of the RTL hit parade, presented at the time by André Thorent. I quote in bulk some names and some corresponding titles: Dave with *Swann's Way*, Gérard Lenorman with *Winter mornings*, Patrick Juvet with *Musica*, C. Jérôme with *Himalaya*, Frédéric François with *Come get lost in my arms*, Michel

Sardou with *Love affliction* and, in addition, thanks to my parents: John William with *Lara's song* and The friends of song with *The Comedians* – which I would later learn, was a composition of Aznavour.

In short, this is what I liked to listen to, the ones to which I would remember the lyrics to with enthusiasm. I can't resist the pleasure of quoting two verses:

– of Dave :
I would gladly go take a walk
Swann's way
To see my first love again
Who gave me a rendezvous
Under the oak
And let herself be kissed on the cheek

– of Sardou :
It runs it runs
Love's affliction
In the hearts of children from 7 to 77 years old
It sings it sings
The insolent river
Uniting in bed
Blond and grey hair

Then, one day – I was 14 years old –, I randomly heard on my favorite radio station, which was broadcasting a show called *Stop or encore*, another quatrain of intro:

Une rob' de cuir comme un fuseau
Qu'aurait du chien sans l'faire exprès
Et dedans comme un matelot
Un' fill' qui tangue un air anglais
––––

A dress of leather like a spindle
Qu'aurait du chien sans l'faire exprès
And inside, like a sailor is
A girl who sings an English air

I had just gotten acquainted with the 5th song, which would become part of my solid knowledge: *C'est extra.*

* * *

It must be said, today, I love singing myself. I used to sing – I still do – with my records and my tapes.

Since the age of 13, at first halted, then developed by growth, my voice got exercised thanks to the aforementioned songs. On the contrary, the 5 base titles, too complicated to be memorized, posed extra problems to my budding singer voice: the notes were too high for me! My young baritone couldn't get used to it yet. It's why – the only two reasons, to tell the truth – I didn't rank Léo Ferré among the singers – translate to: *those whose songs I could easily interpret.*

In college, there were some who followed the same path as me. In high school, on the other hand, I came across some intellectuals of my age, or about who didn't like the same singers I did. Even worse, they despised them, enjoying only their damn "dedicated singers". Horror! I would grit my teeth hearing:
 – It's a commercial song!
 – You don't like dedicated singers? It's a mistake!
 – I want to go to your place to spend the day, but if you give me your Dave bullshit or I don't know who else, I'll leave!

To escape the solitude of the misunderstood listener I had become, I had to make concessions – apparently, at least. I had the good fortune to find at least one friend – the one who left if he had to listen to Dave – who deigned to lend a sympathetic ear to Sardou and Lenorman. One day, at the high school documentation and information center, the same friend pointed to a grossly drawn portrait, with white paint

on the ultramarine blue wall, of an old man with wild hair:
– Who is he? I asked.
– Well, it's Léo Ferré! he said, a little scandalized by my ignorance.
– Ah, yeah! I said. *C'est extra!*

He noticed I liked this title of one of his "dedicated singers" and smiled with ease.

Thanks to you, Léo, I went up in the esteem of a guy I liked, but only to be let royally down as soon as we had the final exam. I don't blame him: life often separates people, even friends. And especially, I owe him for being able to put a face to your voice and your unique "vibe".

Two

Who Are You, Ferré?

A SKING such a question means already knowing the answer. Nevertheless, seeing as the impossible has always fascinated me, I will give this adventure a try.

In fact, Léo Ferré has never really tried to define himself as a person. For the teenager I was and who had the taste of ranking, who liked to put beings and things in places that I would determine for each one, Ferré was a challenge. No, it wasn't a form of narrow-mindedness on my part, as my friends thought; it was rather a desire to set a scene, to provide myself with landmarks, to conclude my own personal exploration of the world.

Ferré, in this regard, was a model, which I soon found out. The sounds, the colors, the images, the impressions, the sensations, nothing could escape him. Everything for him was a material for expression because he had something to say in everything. Thus:

Nous d'une autre trempée et d'une singulière extase
Nous de l'Épique et de la Déraison
Nous des fausses années Nous des filles barrées
Nous de l'autre côté de la terre et des phrases
Nous des marges Nous des routes Nous des bordels intelligents
Ô ma sœur la Violence nous sommes tes enfants

Les pavés se retournent et poussent en dedans[1]

―――

We, of another singular and soaked ecstasy
We, of the Epic and the Derision
We, of fake years We struck through girls
We on the other side of the earth and phrases
We of margins We of roads We of smart brothels
Oh, my sister, Violence we are your children
Pavers turn around and push in

Or:

En même temps que vos impôts
Vous pouvez fair' monter vos bières
Un jour vous n'aurez que la peau
Messieurs les mecs des ministères
Y en a marre
(...)
Monsieur Einstein loin des canons
Croyant travailler pour lui seul
A découvert des équations
Qui vont nous tomber sur la gueule
Y en a marre...[2]

―――

At the same time as your taxes
You can drink your beer
One day you will only have the skin left
Gentlemen of the ministries
We're fed up
(...)
Mr. Einstein get away from the guns
Believing to work for himself alone
He discovered equations

That wil befall us
We're are tired of it...

I remember that Brassens was defined as a « great skimmer of our truths ». In this case, what to say about Ferré? He doesn't skim, in my opinion: he exhibits the pollution of ideas to incite society, those who listen to him, his audience, to do something different. But he never imposes a model or a maxim: Ferré never gave lessons. On the contrary, "to do something differently" would mean for him "do what we want".

This is how he would incite his public to create its own images, their own models, by refusing the pre-established, even anything that equated to forecasts. Indeed, Léo Ferré wasn't a visionary either: he was rather a perpetual analyst of the present.

And this is what he constantly invites us to do.

It's the invitation he just launched me… to push me towards writing this small book!

Three

The Beginning of a Child of the Entertainment

BORN on August 24th, 1916 in Monaco, Léo Ferré could almost be considered as if he had come from the world of entertainment, if his father, employed at the Casino, wouldn't have been so categorical: *"Music doesn't feed a man!"* What to say then about songs and poetry? Still, it's immediately obvious that little Léo would attach himself to the world of the opera – something he will say he owes primarily to his mother, of Italian origin.

Still, it's not thanks to Vivaldi, Rossini and others, Verdi, that Ferré will experience his first lyrical surprise, thanks to a composer who was considered less of an airhead, more bombastic in his conception of art: Ludwig van Beethoven. *The 5th*, the symphony of victory and, for its author, of freedom[3], became a work of reference for Léo Ferré when he heard it for the first time, around 1926.

Thus, his vocation was decided: he will be a musician, and on the way, a poet and a singer. In fact, Léo quickly realized he won't make it easily – it's the least we can say! – through the door of this closed environment, very folded on itself. Moreover, when we know the woes of his favorite composers: Beethoven, Chopin, Ravel, we aren't really surprised! It's why, as soon as he moves to Paris, in the middle of the Occupation, for law studies he'll never finish[4], it's with the songs that he'll create his first weapons.

A bohemian life starts then – the one we might think indispensable to every artist who respects himself. Ferré, member of a small circle of musician friends, composes on the piano and interprets a friend's texts: Germaine Médecin. Still, these soft songs, as he considered them then, do not challenge him. This is why he starts writing songs himself. This is really the only way he could consider being able to make it – even if he has written an *Ave Maria* for organ and cello in 1940, for the occasion of his sister's marriage. He recognizes it himself:

"If I hadn't had a voice and the willingness to do this job, I would have never written."

But the bohemian way doesn't only lie in poetic and musical writing. After having married Odette Shunck, his first wife, in 1943, Léo Ferré will leave Paris to exploit… a farmhouse in Provence! The young couple will live modestly, with a reduced herd of two cows. Ferré doesn't abandon his composition. He will discover, with a certain advance for his time, the baba-cool way of life!

Still, musical centralism requires living in Paris. Léo and Odette will understand it quickly, especially since after a disappointing interview with Charles Trenet, who was a little contemptuous of the young artist, a visit to Édith Piaf will bring him confirmation of the mandatory Parisian life, for any songwriter. The Ferré couple will settle definitively in the capital towards the end of 1946.

***

Was Mr. Ferré father right? Without doubt, since his son and daughter-in-law couldn't claim to live and eat decently through the life of a composer. Moving in, by necessity, with Odette's parents, they will pass from the lean cows of Provence to those of Parisian cabarets! Still, who today would not feel flattered to make their debut at the *Bœuf sur le toit* and at the *Lapin à Gill*, whose prestige is due to many singers, from Bruant to… Ferré, precisely! Various consecrations await Léo: Trenet, who found his music « *not so bad* », will come applaud him.

Jean-Roger Caussimon, a known singer then, will give him texts to set to music. Finally, Renée Lebas will be his first performer, especially singing his famous Paris Canaille:

Paris marlou
Aux yeux de fille
Ton air filou
Tes vieill's guenilles
Et tes gueulantes
Accordéon
Ça fait pas d'rentes
Mais c'est si bon!

A bittersweet observation of the material situation of the Ferré couple!

We observe that Odette will not be able to consider herself as being the money supporter, I dare say: she will leave Léo for good in 1947 – to officially divorce in 1950 –, unable to endure either the bar chair wife lifestyle or, no doubt, her husband's escapade in Martinique, with musician friends. For sure, she had followed him in this sort of exotic adventure, which could suit her frivolous side. But frivolity is not necessarily synonymous with bohemian and the couple will learn it the hard way, as well as other artists, when their producer will flee with their earnings! It's Léo's father who will finance the repatriation of the group. Back in France, Léo won't do much, accepting, with the bittersweet irony that will always characterize him, the departure of his first wife. And, as all artists, he will exorcise this separation by writing a text, which will, at the same time, reaffirm his personality and his will not to deviate from the path he had chosen for himself: *An artist's life*. I only deliver the last verses, to leave aficionados - and others - the pleasure of reading it again or, better, listen to it again:

The Beginning of a Child of the Entertainment

You can take the phonograph
I keep the piano
I continue my life as an artist.

* * *

I'm well placed to know it: the best way for an artist to face adversity, is to oppose the challenge, to oppose the challenge arising, if not from his ambitions, at least from his passion, that nothing and no one can destroy. The artist is like this: we blame him, we mock him, he is vilified, we try to discourage him… he continues on! Like the mythological giant Antée, when the artist is thrown to the ground, he gets up again, stronger.

It's this moral force that will launch Ferré on the even more frantic race of creation. Now, he doesn't have a place to live, he is penniless but he will not let himself be mowed: neither wheat nor oak, it is the reed, which bends in the wind but does not fall more than it lets itself get down. Housed in a small hotel on Street Pré-aux-Clercs, Léo, with the help of songwriter Francis Claude, gradually develops the cabaret *Quod Libet* (= "Which lives") in the cellars of the said hotel, which allows him to be accommodated free of charge as he is an employee. What does it matter, the songs must live! And they will live thanks to Catherine Sauvage, a new Ferré singer – one of the most faithful, actually – then Édith Piaf, whose repertoire will be embellished with *Lovers of Paris*, words and music by friend, Léo.

It is therefore a life of sharing success, at the same time, a life of cabarets, which awaits Ferré. From *Caveau de la Huchette* to *Trois Maillets*, in addition to all those mentioned above, it is doubtless not a Panamanian belligerent who did not see Ferré on scene or one of those who interpreted it.

I a logical manner, if not fortune, at least glory will follow. Singing and being sung, this is the recipe for success: we have nothing without work or without recognition, when we lead an artist's life… Léo will thus go from his first discographic contract with the edition of the

Song of the World, in 1950, to the failure of an opera entitled *La vie d'artiste / An artist's life*, which the Scala of Milan refuses him and even the radio denies. On the contrary, Paris-Inter, ancestor of France-Inter, will give him a show about classical music called *Byzantine music*. He also toured London as a pianist in a film called *The Golden Cage*, but will only appear on film when it's time to see his name on the credits and that's all...

But he has better things to do: first of all, he met Madeleine, his second great love, which will last for more than fifteen years. Then, there's music, songs, always the music and always the songs...

Four

From Odéon to Barclay

*A*LL artists must rise. Today, it's a financial requirement. In the past – let's say, in the 50's-60's –, it was first of all a social ascent, if not more artistic. In fact, it's nice to be an artist, we must live, that is to say, not only to have a bite to eat, but more and foremost, make your art live. Therefore, when making this crucial decision, it's important to know how to choose your partners.

Not only those who compose and interpret with you: Ferré has always known how to choose them and he will never stop recognizing and encouraging his true friends. There are also those who offer you a business partnership; for sure, those will gain money thanks to you, if at least, the public recognized you, then they will know how to propel you, serve as stepping stones and even carrier rockets.

From 1953 to 1968, Léo Ferré will know two: one, Odéon, more innovative and above all, more promising than the Song of the World; the other, Barclay, younger, more dynamic and, despite some pretty deplorable setbacks, more daring.

What does Odéon want? Music, songs. What does Barclay want? The same thing, but more commercial. A world of difference!

Who doesn't remember, especially *Paris Canaille, The poor man's piano, The Guinche, Time of the Tango, Anarchist seed*? It's all of this and even more, seven years of Odéon, from 1953 to 1960. From my point of view, I see a continuity that could have put Ferré among the "poets of the street", the "intellectuals of the left", the "anarchist poets", with a little advance in time, since it is from 1969 that schools programs will integrate them. The street sings, the school drones on. And society, the one who knows the streets a little, purrs so hard that it doesn't listen to people like Ferré, Brassens, Caussimon, Catherine Sauvage, Renée Lebas… although it agrees to "banter" at the cabaret *Chez Patachou* and even in the street with the same Piaf! But let's move on…

For Ferré, recording means arranging then directing, conducting an orchestra. He will practically never succeed by staying at Odéon, then at Barclay. Record companies, with their conservatism and their corporatist imperatives, have nothing to do with his slang of Pershing Boulevard, this space of creation and freedom, this *"very suitable niche for the comfort of dogs, where everything seemed to be organized around the piano."* Even the princely encounters, to which, certainly, Juliette Greco didn't think about when she made this satire. Yet, it is here that Ferré will not hesitate, as a grateful Monegasque citizen, to receive his Serene Highness Prince Rainier himself! Whatever for? For a recital, of course! For sure, it is reduced to one piece, but what a piece: nothing less than the song of Apollinaire's *Mal-Aimé*, set in oratorio by Ferré! It's the cleaver of the last chance: Léo had so far only been refused, especially by the RTF, as was the case with *An artist's life*. But, this time, the friendship of a prince will come in handy: from the Opéra of Monte-Carlo to the radio, where the work will finally impose itself, Ferré will know triumph on his native land.

With Barclay comes the material comfort - purchase of a house in the Eure, an island in Brittany, the castle of Pech-Rigal, renamed "Perdrigal" in the Lot - along with censorship. Nothing is official: it is the publisher himself who censors, not hesitating to pound a record that will be remembered as the *Banned Songs of Léo Ferré: les Rupins, Miss Guéguerre, Thank You Satan, les Quat' cents coups.* Yes! Remember!

It is probably this misadventure that will inspire Léo to have this little diatribe against Eddie Barclay:

"He is kind, he has beautiful cigars, a beautiful mustache and he invites you to lunch every day. He is adorable, Mr. Barclay but he is, nevertheless, a slave!"

What does it matter, since it's that nigger that will make Ferré one of the most popular stars of France!

On my part, I have a feeling that Léo Ferré was lacking, in a way, maturity, especially on the artistic plane. Didn't he know, didn't he know that becoming an artist doesn't mean one has to impose oneself? He who, at the beginning of the 60's, will give a chance to, if we can put it this way, successively to Rutebeuf, Baudelaire, Rimbaud, Verlaine and Aragon by putting their words to music, some on double album, won't he understand then that public recognition, publishers and the world of money comes only from sales, that is to say, the faculty of pleasing while inciting to buy, rather than the creative ability in itself? It's a safe bet that even poets had understood, they, who had never considered the fact of "living" only as an "art of living" and not as a source of food… It is certain that Ferré has, on the contrary, always liked beautiful things, understood by him as part of the dream of the artist and that only money could offer them…

PART II

"LIGHT" or Ferré, a man who grows

Five

A Composer before Anything Else

WE know Léo Ferré as a singer of the street, that is to say « a poet of the street ». We talk about – Queneau, Prévert, Reverdy, Brassens, Renard… – with a little smile – or a little pout – condescending: they're not real poets, according to the general public, for they are, first of all artists, professional hunger breakers who only shine with their words - or even slackers…

Fortunately, Ferré had become a singer! As soon as we sing, we record disks, we sell them and thus, we enter the trade – a desperately modern activity, I could say…

But Léo, we remember, will live the great first shock of his life at the age of 10, when he heard Beethoven's *5th Symphony*. This will determine his vocation.

* * *

Léo Ferré has always considered himself, first of all, a musician or, to say it better, a composer. Singer, poet are labels that he deeply respected, but that he never quite carried inside his being. He is, so to speak, not responsible for how the public viewed him… as all other artists are!

Starting with 1972 the singer or the poet will strive to give the public the image of his personality that he recognized as being the only true one: that of composer. In fact, his complicity with the pianist Paul Castanier, who assisted him in his shows and recordings since 1957, had to have an end in 1973. Many times, the two men had spats because the piano accompaniment on stage – the only form of musical accompaniment Ferré considered suitable for his concerts – didn't satisfy Léo anymore, becoming more and more demanding in this regard, downright manic - but what artist isn't?

In short, Castanier was soon marked with an infamous label: *he was no longer playing Ferré!* He seemed to be simply an act of presence on stage, hidden behind the instrument-furniture! The pianist Castanier and the lyricist Maurice Frot signed with Ferré a contract that will tie all of them together till May 1973; they will never renew it.

* * *

So Léo finds himself alone, first in life – his father dies, Madeleine divorces him for good[5] – then on stage, where he now accompanies himself to the piano, something he had not done since his debut. Still, sometimes, we notice that in concerts, he takes solo piano alternations with pre-recorded orchestral. In fact, Ferré could not afford the cost of an accompanying orchestra, having as primary concern to not increase the price of tickets. The composer wants to remain popular, in the most democratic sense, going to the most proletarian side of the term. He will never suffer that his shows can only be seen by rich people. When you know his mentality well, this doesn't surprise you…![6]

Otherwise, Léo Ferré starts from this time to assume the arrangements of his recording himself, so the whole orchestration part. The double album *Alone on stage – Léo Ferré 73* is testimony, although inconclusive for Ferré because, if he actually made the arrangements himself, he is not at all convinced by the aesthetics of this record, to the point of insisting near Barclay that the double album be taken out of the catalogue. Pity! There are beautiful titles in it: *The oppression, Night and Day, Don't sing death* – not all sung though: *Preface*[7] and *There's nothing anymore* are long texts read or recited with musical accompaniment. Ferré fans be assured: the double album was reissued in 1999 under the title *There's nothing anymore*.

Justly: let's talk about those texts a little, sung or not, which constitute, according to certain critics pieces of anthology. For my part, if I were a record publisher, I would make a compilation, or even a box of four or five CDs at least. In addition to the two titles mentioned above, I would also place *la Chanson du Mal-Aimé* – but it is true that the text is from Apollinaire –, *Métamec, Zaza, Muss es sein? Es muss sein!* and above all *Death...Death...Death* with its conclusion that pays in the "shocking poetic", I would say: *"JE VOUS LAISSE LA VUE IMPRISE SUR LA MERDE"*/ «*I LEAVE YOUR VIEW IMPRINTED ON THE SHIT*» – in capital letters!

The public wasn't mistaken: it always welcomed these hyper-long texts with skepticism. No doubt it was not happy to see Ferré fight with his piano as he did with his words. A compilation of these titles would probably be a commercial disaster. On my part, I would flee these concerts in which the artist takes, somehow, pretext of a poster announcing a "concert" to put his audience very brutally in contact with his moods. It's not an excuse to do it.
Is it true, Ferré, what... in the end? What came over you?
If you were sick of everything, as it seemed to be then, why didn't you just give us other texts, as juicy as the others, as harmonious as *He's had enough, The life of an artist, Pépée, With time* or, precisely, you expressed some weariness and sadness from your life? Why hit so hard on the words and music that had done nothing to you?

Well...! I don't want to close this chapter on a disillusioned note. I will mention a feat you did in February 1975, where you conducted an orchestra while singing (!) given during a tour in Switzerland, this show was titled *Music often takes me as... love does*. From this tour, an album will be released entitled *Ferré mute*, where you also directed interpretations of Beethoven and Ravel. But making a dream come true isn't without risk: the critics will pretend that *"Beethoven murders Ferré"*, which seems a clever inversion, almost a spoonerism, in a way… This is the ransom of a successful singer and poet!

Six

The Poet, The Poets

Please allow me, to start this new chapter, by adding a personal memory.

One Friday evening, I was watching in front of my little screen at *Apostrophes*, a still well-known program by Bernard Pivot. That evening, the guardian of culture on channel 2 had brought together several singers rather than writers, especially Serge Gainsbourg and Guy Béart – note in passing that Léo Ferré wasn't present, either he had not been invited, or he had declined the invitation. Still, had he been there, he would not have failed to react against a virulent apostrophe of «the man with the cabbage head», who defined the song as «a minor art» in relation to poetry. Guy Béart, present on set, rebelled violently. A quarrel followed that Bernard Pivot had trouble appeasing... But what would the man with the lion's head think?

I have already said it: Ferré didn't consider himself primarily a poet and a singer, but a composer[8]. It is, without a doubt, the reason for which his opinion would have been, at the same time, more nuanced and above all, more complete, more reflective, more polysomic than that of Gainsbourg, beyond the indignation of Béart too. Let's see instead:

"*If The Flowers of Evil still grow on the threshold of Verlain's poetry, it is that their deep rhetoric, as we have said, encumbered all that was done in the garden very close to them. How to look at a sick sky, a stealthy woman, how to smell a heavy perfume, how to be oneself in front of the cynical beauty of 1857 flowers, when you're a young poet, in the shop of hyphenation and hiatus, and all the rest of the formal imperatives that make the poet first and foremost a versifier, a worker."*

Thus, Ferré would not have defined poetry as a « major art », to make fun of Gainsbourg, but rather like the quintessence of all arts. Baudelaire, according to Léo, had found a way of expression that would have been complete without "rhetoric" or "formal imperatives". Of course, he is not the first to have rebelled against everything that made the poet "a versifier, a worker": Baudelaire wanted to create the poem in prose with *Spleen of Paris*, Rimbaud with *A season in hell*, Ponge with *Proèmes*... The list is not exhaustive!

* * *

To be more precise, let's consider what the word « poet » represents for Léo Ferré:

> *Ce sont de drôl's de typ's qui vivent de leur [plume*
> *Ou qui ne vivent pas c'est selon la saison*
> *Ce sont de drôl's de typ's qui traversent la lune*
> *Avec des pas d'oiseaux sur l'aile des [chansons...*[9]
> ———
> There are funny men who live by their [pen
> Or who do not live according to season
> There are funny men who cross the moon
> With bird steps on the wings of [songs...

The terms "*funny men*" are perfectly suitable, let us acknowledge, to the poets mentioned above, especially Verlaine, who was just good at being cared for by one or the other, without having ever worked in his life, and Rimbaud, stray teenager and exotic adventurer. On the contrary, they don't really suit, especially if we consider the connotations from the 4th verse, to poets like Baudelaire, a small bourgeois busy squandering the paternal inheritance, or like Aragon, from an affluent background and defending a totalitarian "ideal"…!

On my part, I considered as "*funny men*" most contemporary poets, those I had the chance to meet, to work with: whether or not they have a food income – it's their only ounce of wisdom –, they constantly publish words, texts, forms of writing and ideas that contribute to a perpetual creation of poetry. It is undoubtedly those that Ferré would have preferred among all. There is no doubt he knew many…

***

On the other hand, Ferré's poetic work, if we want to analyze it that way, seeks to create a harmony between words, images, colors and sounds[10]. To do this, he is mainly inspired by Rimbaud. His song *Of all the colors* resumes in his own way the theme(s) developed by Rimbaud in the sonnet *Vowels*:

A black, E white, I red, U green, O blue: vowels,
I shall tell, one day, of your mysterious origins

Ferré took up this project that Rimbaud could not realize:

Of all the green colors if you prefer
To go into your life when it despairs
To escape the noise when it [exaggerates
And when it meets a field of shade at the end of your sun
When the perfumes, jealous of your profound aroma
Arrange themselves to throw their signals round
And to say that the virtuous woods of autumn
Are asked to descend and give alms
From their grief put in pills and in sleep

To create a poetic music with colors was therefore a very personal theme. Here, poetry is a painting, not a text. *"And the music?"* Gainsbourg would say. It is not forgotten: the music that Ferré gave to many poems by Baudelaire, Rimbaud, Verlaine or Aragon gives back to the verb "to grant" its main meaning, that of putting in agreement, in relation, in concordance, in counterpoint, in short, in harmony the words, images and colors with music.

This is how the slow and throbbing rhythms accorded to Rimbaud's[11] *Vowels* and Baudelaire's[12] *Correspondances* weighing on the images and thus, wish to increase, in a crescendo, both musical and visual, the appearance and brilliance of colors, up to a sort of burst. Léo Ferré so created, without suspecting it, one of the first effects of what is now called *virtual*.

To my knowledge, only Jean-Michel Jarre, who frequently spoke of the same intentions, has been capable of obtaining this type of three dimensional creation, especially at his concert in Paris La Défense in 1990.

* * *

In 1961, Léo Ferré was the first one to sing Louis Aragon, imitated later by Brassens and Jean Ferrat. The album *Léo Ferré sings Aragon* resumes rhythms, either throbbing or resolutely modern, extracts of great poems, the most known being *the Red Poster, Is that how men live* and *I sing to pass the time*. Tell us, Léo, what were your intentions, really?

"I met Aragon in his book[11], at the very heart of his words. I read it with my hands chained to the keyboard and to my voice. Let's get this straight: this is not a formula, nor an image, but the expression of a technique. The verse of Aragon is, apart from any evocation, connected to the music."

It is, therefore, natural that you "plugged" onto Aragon. You did the same thing with Rimbaud:

"Rimbaud, he is light words. He is the impatient tide that seems made for you to absorb with a look."

Thus, with each meeting of a poet, Ferré felt "chained to the keyboard", that is to say, to that of his piano. The poets took Léo in, and he spoke in the tone they used with him. So, if Ferré celebrated the poets, the poets have, in a way, forced Ferré to reveal himself to his own eyes while putting their verses to music.

* * *

No wonder, therefore, that Ferré was no more authoritative in the musical adaptation of poems than they would have appreciated the academism in which their work had sometimes been drowned:
"It has become customary to write, in textbooks of literature, that the verse is self-sufficient and that the syllables sing, that the rhyme or assonance show the contours of verbal melody. Apart from purely phonetic research, the poet writes words, their music, if any, does not go without a certain internal rhythm. Thus, the Alexandrine is magnificent, the octosyllabic is less so, and the four syllable one seems to yield more to the desire to speak than to sing."

Protest, sometimes taking on the appearance of a profession of faith – *"I don't believe so much in the verse's music, but in a certain form conducive to the meeting of the verb and the song. »* –, can look like a disillusioned satire: « *They looted you, Baudelaire (...) Poetry has muzzled you in a labeled genius, odorless with beautiful and consistent speeches that must be made about you during an unimportant distribution of prizes at the high school of Nevers."*[12]

That's why I'll finish this chapter by clarifying: many language teachers - from Nevers high school and elsewhere, rest assured, Léo! - have gone above and beyond the academic discourse, leaving themselves open to be reprimanded, immobilized on the rungs of their careers or even knock on the door when they wanted to put the study of Baudelaire, including – the beautiful, the untouchable author of *The Flowers of Evil*! – to the Ferré mix[13]. This may also concern the study of other poets. The voice of the State will always be right, Léo, when it is represented by the creators of school programs and especially by those who watch over its execution, putting on their blinkers and sharpening their stupid and mean critical sense.

In this respect, Léo Ferré was an authentic *seer*, who had the advantage of being free.

Let's hope he had enough followers to be the cause of a force that one day will *overtake* the Mammoth and forever eliminate the Dinosaurs!

Seven

The Singer, The Singers

COMPOSER, poet with polymorphic conceptions... So, was Léo Ferré not a singer? But, of course he was: according to Aragon, *"he renders a service to poetry whose impact is still poorly calculated, putting at the disposal of the new reader, a novice reader, poetry coupled with musical magic. (...) Literary history will have to be written a little differently because of Léo Ferré."*[14]

Thus, to know Ferré, the poet, one must also know Ferré, the singer, it is essential. By "knowing", I mean, to practice, to listen, to know to appreciate while consuming without moderation. It's Aragon again who found the best formula: to discover Ferré, the singer, you shouldn't be just a listener, but also a *"novice reader". Reader by ear*

It's an undeniable fact: Léo Ferré's career begins with music and organizes itself around it. According to him, of course, song, music, poetry, painting, even photography, practically constitute an inseparable whole[15]. Still, he himself, at the height of his glory, had to recognize the predominance of song.

Moreover, it's with the singers that he'll have the most contact with, from his debut to the end. For sure, he won't be one of the young prodigies of the stage that Mrs. Piaf tried to launch, since she only sang from him *Lovers of Paris*. He will even follow - wrongly, I think - the advice he received from Trenet in 1941: to not risk singing his own songs.

This is how Renée Lebas, Catherine Sauvage and Juliette Gréco will become his favorite interpreters. It's for the same reason, most probably, he'll sing the songs of others, especially those of Jean-Roger Caussimon… to get his own place, virtually at the same time!

So, with Léo Ferré, there were two periods in music: Ferré provider of songs and Ferré performer of his own compositions.

Still, let's open a first parenthesis: Léo, indefinable by personal choice, let's say, frequently straddled these two conceptions. The most important example is his reunion with Jean-Roger Caussimon, in April 1985, that is, forty years after their first meeting. This fidelity in the lyrical art will be concretized by an album entitled *The Hooligans* and subtitled *Léo Ferré sings Jean-Roger Caussimon.* A TV show named *Nights of absence*, the title of one of the songs, will promote the work. It is regrettable, however, that administrative delays didn't allow the program to be broadcast before May 2, 1986 for Caussimon could never see it: he had died since October 20th of the previous year.

As for the second parenthesis, it will open on the winks that Ferré sometimes launched to his main passion: orchestral music. Thus, some of his less well-known albums will contain pieces of the classical repertoire that he will create and lead himself with the passion we know him capable of. Let's remember *I give you*, a CBS album from 1976, that apart from six songs, contains Beethoven's *Coriolan Overture*, directed by Ferré, who leads the Orchestra of Milan[16] for the occasion. Beethoven is also doubly honored in this album with a text recited, in his own composition *Muss es sein? Es muss sein!*

I will tell, to make you laugh a little, the little story of this piece: Beethoven, having for debtor *Herr* Dembscher, who owed him 50 florins, claimed the sum from him. The man, rather annoyed by this debt, asked: *"Muss es sein ? –* Is it necessary?" To which, Beethoven replied: *"Ja, es muss sein! –* Yes, it is!" with the magnanimity that characterized him. It was he who later became the debtor of his friend since he owed him the music, composed immediately on that air that trotted in his head. *Muss es sein? Es muss sein!*, a piece for quartet, which ends with: *"Heraus mit dem Beutel!"* – Get your wallet out!"[17]

Finally, let's talk about the entirely musical album *Ferré mute... directed by Ravel and Ferré*. Containing *Love, The Death of Wolfs* and *Piano Concerto for the Left Hand* by Ravel, he also resumes in instrumental version *Muss es sein? Es muss sein!* Always anxious to surprise his audience, Ferré duplicated this album with another title *Pia Colombo sings Ferré 75*. This Italian interpreter did, in fact, a great service to Léo because his contract with Barclay prevented him from recording his own songs among his own productions[18]. So it is Pia Colombo who sang the texts composed on the aforementioned music…

In short, the singer and the singers were all united like the fingers of a hand.

To Louis Aragon who said that it would be necessary to reinvent, to redefine poetry after Léo Ferré, one would be tempted to answer that music would also find this redefinition very much to his liking… not to mention the listeners' taste!

Eight

With Time...

∽✿∽

"MUSIC and words, I did it in two hours", declared Léo talking about *Avec le temps / With Time*, his most known "hit" with *C'est extra*. It's natural: a settling of accounts is always done as quickly as possible, so as not to leave anything behind. This song puts an end to a happy time. Thus:

The heart, when it stops beating
It's not worth going any further
You have to let it go and that's fine.

An advice, maybe… Afterwards, it is above all the very poignant regrets of this period of love that ended badly, as evidenced by these verses, among the most evocative:

The other to whom we gave the boot and jewelry
For one who would sell his soul for pennies
In front of all of this
Who dragged ourselves along like street dogs…

So, a humiliation[19]. More like an internal massacre… to which Ferré would sometimes add that of the text and his song during future concerts.

For sure, there is enough to be annoyed with when a song of this kind becomes a great popular success. But, probably it wasn't necessary to record it first on a single 45 type, created in 1970: formerly, this disk format wasn't, as quickly thereafter, a hit-parade success, but simply a more economical production. Thus, the 70's will see the legend of the 45 type, as headlines of media – "hits"! Léo Ferré probably hadn't foreseen this very questionable evolution, which was not so strange after all, as we can say, to the premature death of the 45 type...[20]

* * *

With time, is also a book, composed and left unfinished by Léo Ferré and the photograpger Hubert Grooteclaes.

The work will be finished, after the disappearance of its first two creators, by Patrick Buisson. *"We discover a Ferré totally writer-poet, in control of the verb and the deep song"*, writes Luc Vidal[21]. Even better: *"We discover an authentic photographer-poet."*[22]

Primitively titled *The eternity of the moment*, the work received the title *With time* by the will of Oak editions: the commercial aspect of the "hit" probably had a lot to say in this decision! The success of the book will not contradict this conception, as long as talent is, of course, in no way affected. There was never anything overrated in the collaboration of the two creators. I won't say anything more, leaving it to the true fans to discover for themselves this unusual work...

With time will only be included in a 30 cm album in 1972, by Barclay's decision, who created an ultimate compilation titled *Léo Ferré's Love Songs*. This uninspired title offers a frame that can only negatively affect the artist's work. But commerce always speaks first and it is with this intention that Barclay, then in charge of Ferré productions, will produce this album which, from many points of view, isn't really an album. Even the presence of an already old title: *The artist's life*, doesn't manage to retrieve this disc from the pool of simple consumer goods. No luck, Léo!

For my part, I don't distinguish myself from the general public since I, too, fell in love *With time...*

I'll have the opportunity, later on, to evoke in the same way the history and the future of another song which, like this one, sings permanently in my ear.

PART III

"GALBE" / "CONTOUR" or Ferré, a man who indisposes

Nine

Love-Anarchy

F OR you, Léo, *"Anarchy is the political shape of despair."* Were we to understand you, anarchy can therefore represent at least two essential things:

Primo: desperation erected in a political program. Thus, the desperate people of the world will unite hands to shout their revolt against a society they cannot accept. What's new here? Quite simply, the fact that the human being isn't born, it seems, to produce, that is to say, to manufacture objects, to sell them and to buy them - to live by it and for the power of the currency. For sure, this is the classic pattern of any human society based on industrial development, because it knows no other alternative, except that of the "good savage", dear to the Utopians of the eighteenth century. So, anarchy doesn't represent a fight? But of course it does: *"So it's up to us* [the artists] *to prepare your rebellion. We write the psychology of revolt with feather techniques. We walk on the belly of tyrants with lightly, we give the alarm with cries of birds."*[23] The politicians of Anarchy, so to say, of despair, are the artists themselves. Anarchy is then created for the benefit of the masses through art. It becomes an art, just like Oscar Wilde had expressed it in regards to life.

Secundo: politics erected in despair. It's the most negative way, it seems, and the least productive to serve anarchy. Politics always claims to regulate life and society affairs. If it becomes desperation, it resembles a fight already lost. As such, it's a form of political suicide. It can then be, either a "murder by suicide of politics", that is, to deny it as a way to bring happiness by activating its suppression, or to erect suicide in politics: society will live as quickly as possible since its march towards death will be programmed. It's without doubt, actually, the case for a number of political systems, whose end, history knows. Will anarchy have the same fate?

It's still suicide, ally of despair – and vice versa – that was Ferré's lot from the beginning of 1968. In reality, Perdrigal castle is inhabited by a jealous woman, who had learned about her husband's affair with Mary, his new muse. Enraged to find herself alone in the middle of a whole menagerie, Madeleine takes terrible measures: first, the two monkeys, Pépée and Zaza, which Madeleine Ferré had nevertheless wished the presence of, against the opinion of Léo, originally, then the pig, considered another pet, will be sacrificed. The other animals, cows and hens, will be given to the neighbors. Returning from a gala, Léo will find an empty space, Madeleine herself having fled Perdrigal. Never will this massacre or flight be forgiven to Madeleine.

Fleeing Perdrigal himself, Ferré will know from then on a wandering life with his two faithful friends: Maurice Frot and Paul Castanier. All three will form a kind of Illustrious Theater in the manner of Molière, traveling the roads of France, giving concerts here and there. Actually, a rather anarchic way to perpetuate a career!

It is rather in the news that it will continue: no doubt against his will, Léo Ferré will become one of the spearheads of the protest movement of May 68. Recognized on the terrace of a Parisian cafe on May 10th, Ferré will refuse to join the protesters, but will support them in his writings and his songs. Indeed, we had already noticed his propensity to provoke, by singing about things that disturb, like *The Red Poster* of the album *Ferré sings Aragon* in 1961. Then, what to say about the recording of 1968 – that some entitled *Summer of 68* when it had no original title? It is, if not a plea, at least an illustration for the rioters:

Comme une fille
La rue s'déshabille
Les pavés s'entassent
Et les flics qui passent
Les prennent sur la gueule

———

Like a woman
The street takes her clothes off
The cobblestones pile up
And the passing cops
Take them on the mouth

The same rioters recognized you, Léo, because you had already claimed in a previous album that you had *No God No Master*:

These woods that are said to be of justice
And that grow in tortures
And to furnish the sacrifice
With the fir for the service
This procedure which watches
Those whom society rejects
Under the pretext that they may have
NO GOD, NO MASTER

Here it is, the formula dear to the anar – or to the *anarchists*! This is probably why we don't find it in a previous song: *Anarchist seed*, which, on the "anarchistic" plan, disappoints more than it disturbs:

I'm told that I grew
Below a gallow
Where my grandpa
Was already swinging
With a necklace

A braided necklace
From hemp it was
A damn scarf
From an anarchist seed

No, but really, Léo, this cartoonist image can't convince us of your opinions. Honestly, we – it's in the plural – prefer *They voted*:

À leur chanter des tas d'chansons
Dies irae et toute la clique
Les morts en veine de migration
Se sont levés avec des triques
Ils sont allés au cinéma
Voir la Symphonie Pathétique
On dit qu'ils n'ont pas aimé ça
Les morts n'aiment pas la musique
Ils ont voté… et puis après?
————

Singing them lots of songs
Dies irae and the whole gang
The dead in vein of migration
Got up with cudgels
They went to the movies
To see the Pathetic Symphony
They say they didn't like it
The dead do not like music
They voted … and after that?

As well as *The Anarchists*:

There is not one in a hundred and yet they exist
Most Spaniards will know why
But in Spain they are not understood

*The Anarchists
They gathered everything
Some clouts and some stones
They screamed so loudly
That they can still scream
They have their hearts in front
And their dreams in the middle
Their souls all gnawed
By damned ideas*

If there's something about the Spanish, it's surely for this reason:

*In the bellies of the Spaniards
There are arms ready ready
Who wait*

By the way, those you could not convince with one of the songs, the best one interpreted, from *Summer 68*, it's the anarchists and the baba-cool, with *C'est extra*![24] Anyway, you had already said it: *"I'm gonna make a hit!"* You won the bet, my friend! If *Summer 68* still remained your best sold album, it's because of that "hit", the grandiose text and arrangements that are very *Sixties*! Jean-Michel Defaye did his work well, especially adding the Hammond organ which, already in that time, contributed to the success of the famous *Whiter Shade Of Pale* of the mythical group *Procol Harum*. You were then in your own time, Léo: it caught up with you… and the music trend too, whether you like it or not, as you exceeded your own intentions!

The personal desperation, very personal even, has not been forgotten:

*J'voudrais avoir les mains d'la mort
Pépée
Et puis les yeux et puis le cœur
Et m'en venir coucher chez toi*

Ça chang'rait à mon décor
On couche toujours avec des morts (ter)

———

I would like to have the hands of death
Chick
And then the eyes and then the heart
And come sleep at your house
It would change my decor
We always sleep with dead people

Subsequently, the compositions of Ferré will become, it seems to me, less and less "anarchic" – or more and more according to Ferré and perhaps according to Madeleine since she will one day go up on the stage of the cabaret Don Camillo, in Saint-Germain-des-Prés, to slap her ex-husband in public! Either way, it's not essential: he truly forgot it, since he moved to Tuscany with the true love of his life: Mary.

Then, Léo Ferré goes on tours, international now, since there he is in Québec at the beginning of the 70's, where he'll record with rockers. Did he wish to meet the famous Jimmy Hendrix? Maybe, not sure. Anyway, no offense to uninformed historiographers, they'll never meet. Still, Ferré, back in France, will participate in the public recognition of a French group, brand new, really beautiful: *Zoo*. He'll take them in an album: *Solitude*, on the stage at the Olympia.

I open a parenthesis: it was around this same time - I was 11 years old - that I had the opportunity, while watching one of my favorite shows on a Thursday afternoon, to discover the same band. I still remember its leader and the group's history, as he put it:

"We had a music teacher who, one day annoyed, told us: "You play like animals!" It's what gave us the idea for the name of our group. Later, the name was transformed in English: Zoo[25]*."*

Léo had joined what was then called "pop music", that is, the rock who wanted to work with the legendary *Moody Blues*. Disappointed not to have met them on his way, at least to compose[26], he dedicated

C'est extra, making two nostalgic references to *"Moody Blues who sing at night"* and to *"Moody blues swaying"*…!

* * *

Then, what is anarchy for you, Léo?

It's also love, since you only knew with Mary the joy of being a father? To the point of showing the picture of your son Mathieu as a child, on one of your albums?[27]

Is it the challenge? How to arrive at the concert in a Rolls Royce, as from a legend with no foundation? You loved beautiful cars, we already know, but probably not the Rolls…

It's this 600-page treatise you wanted to write as early as 1970 - rather than finishing your autobiographical novel: *Benoît Misère*[28], the same year? The idea came to you, since this treatise, left only in a project state, still aroused a lot of notes found after your death…

Was it your support for the left side, then? But probably not on the extreme left, since many of its small groups, certainly among the most detestable, haven't recognized in you *"a true revolutionary"*?

No, Léo, Anarchy in you was summed up in its great initial, the same as Art. It's the refusal of all authority, but especially any school, any artistic trend - at least when possible… In any case, it's the refusal to make it into a doctrine, a party: *"The black flag is beautiful, but it's still a flag."* Your son will say it after you: *"Anarchy, it's him. (…)It's a solitary thing. Two, that works. Three, it's war, a mess."* Did you become Sartrean, to the point of discovering that hell is represented by the others?

Ten

The Producer

Till September 1976, Léo Ferré didn't have the right to publish his songs or, so to speak, record his records where he wanted, as he wanted. Sure, the exam at the SACEM, which required any postulant songwriter to go through this door to have the right to sign texts, melodies and arrangements, had been lived - and it wasn't a bad thing! But the contrasting truth remained always the same: Ferré was tied to Eddie Barclay, which cost him, as we have already seen, if not setbacks, at least great frustrations, unacceptable to a spirit like his: *"I was tired of being a commodity for producers..."*

September 1976 is therefore a blessed date for a sexagenarian Léo, more and more inclined to claim his thirst for freedom, even if only commercially. It's by becoming his own producer, Ferré will realize his dream in full and live his music even in the spiritual sense of the term, one could say. Before, music lived through him. From then on, music and him will become one!

His Italian ancestry, on his mother's side, as well as various economic circumstances will then encourage him to record his future records in Tuscany, where he lives with Mary. He explained himself thus:

"With the Orchestra of Milan[29], I produce a band, in Italy preferably, it's less expensive than in France and I get a license for it wherever I want. I no longer sign anywhere and with just anyone..."

Ferré is now a star, even if he doesn't acknowledge it. The distribution of his records won't pose any problems: the American CBS and even, again, Eddie Barclay want to support him, the first starting with 1976 with the album *Je te donne / I give you*, the second, two years later than the first: *It's six o'clock here... and noon in New York*. Still, the "nigger" Barclay[30] still has unacceptable conditions for Ferré: he refuses to erase from his catalogue the public recording from Olympia 72. So it's RCA who will distribute in 1980 *The violence of boredom* then, two years later, the monumental *Ludwig-The Imaginary-The Drunken Boat*.

This great album, unique within the Ferré discography, can be considered as the culmination of his work as a writer-composer. It is really a musical triptych, like it had never been recorded before then, and who knows how to harmoniously play with various musical styles. *Ludwig*, tribute to Beethoven, an idol of Ferré's since childhood, is a set of works for strings, dominated by guitars and harp. *The Imaginery* is dominated by percussions. As for *The drunken boat*, eponymous of the famous poem of Rimbaud, puts it to music mostly by voice, which also predominates in the other three pieces: *Of all the colors, Love dies* and *The Sorgue*. All critics agree to recognize the exceptional quality of this triptych, while regretting that it is not so known...[31]

Anyway, such a musical work seems to make Ferré a liar when he says: *"I am careful since I have children."* A monumental work is an expensive one. Moreover, as previously said, this work won't be the best known among the Ferré recordings. To this commercial risk comes the one that Mary takes after giving birth to Mathieu and Marie-Cécile, valiantly pushing towards completion her third pregnancy: Manuella, third and last child of the new Ferré couple, born on January 26th, 1978, one month before the death of her maternal grandmother.

If I talk about it, it's good to show that Léo had chosen to live his life as an artist fully, that is to say, dangerously: an artist is a perpetual investor, who composes, interprets, produces if he can and wins over the public if he wants. We make do with what we have, but we always advance. Moreover, we never hesitate, like Ferré has always done, paying for himself while touring the roads of France in meeting a more and more faithful and conquered public. It's a chance, and at the same time, a feat: to my knowledge, only Henri Salvador wanted to push the song and the show to their last limits, while hoping that they will not be the last! As for Léo, he will conduct two concerts in one go at two different locations, in May 1983:

"*Léo Ferré broke a world record that no singer can claim to date. Without opponent, at the Olympic Games of Music, he would be a gold medalist!*", *Ici-Paris* says.

"The old lion of the song" never ceases to surprise us!

Eleven

Léo-Benoît, Ferré-Misère

*L*ÉO FERRÉ is an *author*: it is, as an artist, the best qualification that, for my part, I can give him – notice I avoided talking about *labels*: he would surely not have liked that word at all.

The majority of the authors I had the pleasure of meeting are novelists. Léo Ferré isn't an exception, since he also wrote a novel: *Benoît Misère*. For the record, the book is supposed to tell the childhood of its author, especially his experience in *«prison»* that is to say from the pension at Saint-Charles College in Bordighera, Italy. Becoming number 38 of said boarding school, young Léo uses, it seems, the same strategy as Napoleon Bonaparte when he was a student at the college of Autun, then at the military school of Brienne: he takes refuge in solitude and reading. Ferré will add music.

The novel will be started on November 25th, 1956, while Ferré lives in Paris, boulevard Pershing. That's when a slow and long work starts, since the work will only be finished on June, 19th 1970 – fourteen years of writing! It's true that the artist had much to do…!

I spoke earlier about the traumatic experience at the pension. Perhaps I was wrong to quote this negative aspect, which may immediately discourage fans of beautiful novels. But everything is repairable! Let us quote rather the most beautiful experiences of a Monegasque childhood bursting with sun and scents "à l'italienne". Let's take this into account:

"*On days when Magdalena from the laundry room was making ravioli, her workbench was near the furnace which Chino then confided to her for observation. I, my chin close to the table, I looked on. I watched this woman instructing the stuffing of beef and Swiss chard, then kneading it with an egg and grated parmesan, not too slow, not too fast, and then dividing into small balls that she settled on the large dough ironed like a silk shirt which one would eat, thin paste, but strong and which, turned over, was inserted on the stuffing, the embossing more precisely, forming small closed and detailed hat like shapes with the help of the roulette which made the edges edentulous and enough to satisfy the eye when the fork would prick in their felt.*"

This novel will be published by Robert Laffont in October 1970. Léo Ferré had become a star, the book carried a strip of paper mentioning *"the first novel by Léo Ferré"*. This mention had more to do with advertising than the truth of the matter, since this novel will remain the only exploration the composer will make in this precise field.

Presentations made by the press will be dictated above all by the geographical situation of periodicals. Thus, Parisians will have this sinister title to read: *"The story of one of those punks, like the punks you see in jail at age 9"* – certainly, we probably wouldn't dare write the same things! On the other hand, the aspect of a "sunny childhood" will notably mark the Southerners.

The book's structure, which doesn't really respect a classical novel, since the sixteen chapters don't follow one another and only reproduce "seen things"– or rather, felt –will have made more ink flow than the "things" themselves. *Benoît Misère* will be compared to Alain Fournier's *Grand Meaulnes*, Daudet's *Small Things* and the defiant novels and stories of Pagnol[32]. It is indeed always easier to refer to other works to analyze a new one, almost erasing the newness it brings! This is the way of language teachers, as they are "trained" today. It is by comparing one to the other that schoolboys are encouraged to compose. No one will have the right to frankly say what he thinks of this or that book that he discovered with more or less joy, given the atmosphere in which this discovery will take place...

Myself, I couldn't control it. *Mea culpa*: I was a language teacher for almost fifteen years. I am not yet rid of all the miasma that I was forced to contaminate my students with. That's why I'm going to take advantage of this chapter to get rid of it, to "make it go away" once and for all.

It's not really important to know, basically, if this book is autobiographical. It is not, it seems, since the author wanted to « tell the story of a certain childhood »[33]. Me, I would like to say it is. But I will stand by my belief that "Léo-Benoît" is a true character, who wants to "testify"... but to what profit?

For his own, first of all. In my opinion, the best proof, is the incompleteness of the book. Do we stop a life when we go into adulthood? If the answer is yes, we must believe that Ferré also refused to, like many, make a review of his first years – nor that of his main character. *"Then Misère got up from his table, closed his typewriter, lit a cigarette and went out. He went to a tomb and talked to it..."* If that's what this is about, then it's that the age of the man the author refers to is a kind of personal death, that of ideas maybe... or rather that of appearances: Léo Ferré was not a man to live like a kind of a plastic-coated celebrity; that's why he always fought against "the image" that stardom – of which he could not escape – could have given him. Starting from there, he refused to go with the trend, society, what those times wanted to give him, taking even the appearance of the most common objects:

"I don't only exist to rave about everything I create: when I see a poplar, it is I who give it life, and it dies as soon as I am dead to him." Without doubt, Ferré managed to get out of Plato's cave! I make my excuses, I'm still playing the teacher... Or not really: even a teacher can be passionate about certain things.

Finally, Léo Ferré comes out of his story by the very mechanics of his writing: *"And I'm only a writer who writes".* This is what I prefer, as an editor...!

Me too, I am according to things I have witnessed. I mentioned the ones that struck me the most in *Benoît Misère*, while sorting them out, so as not to go beyond the scope of this little book. This wasn't my objective.

So, I conclude this chapter by stating my own theory: this novel that is really not one is still autobiographical, at least if one wants to be content with a somewhat impoverishing term. To be more precise, I would say that *Benoît Misère* is a "contemplative" work, that is to say an essay on oneself, on one's thoughts - not only that of the author himself. He who reads the book thinks, without closing it or throwing it away. The reader reflects on himself by trying to see between Ferré's lines. This was, without doubt, Léo's intention.

To sum it up, *Benoît Misère* may be the ancestor of the collection of books *"to which you are the hero of"*…!

Twelve

Memory and the Sea

IN his new role as producer, Léo Ferré will put the base of a publishing house in 1992: *Memory and the sea*, eponymous of one of his most beautiful songs and run today by his son Mathieu, who is actively involved in perpetuating the paternal memory by editing and re-editing all the documents, written and oral, corresponding to the work of the songwriter.

* * *

Allow me to comment first on the song itself.

Memory and the sea was created in 1962, recorded in the album *Love Anarchy Ferré 70*. Like many others of Léo's[34] songs, it knew at least two versions, on paper and on disk.

Thus, the collection of texts *Testament phonographe* presents it in five stanzas of sixteen verses each. The first sung version, the one recorded in 1970, appears in the collection *The bad Seed*, to which Léo Ferré put the finishing touches to before dying.

It should be noted, however, that this long text, frequently reworked and amplified, will contain by itself no less than seven songs. It will know various different titles: *Songs of Fury, Guesclin, The sea's memory, Words, FLB, The Black Sea, Geometrically empty, Christie* and finally, *Margins*!

So, Léo Ferré played with his texts just like as a child with his cubes would – with a difference though, the cubes were not always the same!

It was necessary to pay special homage to this multifaceted, multi-sonic, shapely text… as it alone multiplies by seven Léo Ferré's talent!

* * *

Memory and the sea as a publishing house is therefore thirty years younger than the song. Its story is tied with the word « necessity »: like many artists who "move up" – meaning: who bring in the big bucks – Léo Ferré often had trouble with his publishers, including Barclay, against whom he won a lawsuit.

The expression "give up your rights" is always dangerous, although it has nothing on its colleague: "recover rights".

When a publisher keeps an artist who "moves up", he keeps him on a tight leash. Consequently, he knows how to play with words in publishing contracts, in order to ensure the longest possible hold on the titles that sell best. On this subject, we know that Léo Ferré's best sold record is *Summer 68*. These risky and abusive clauses, with the famous "right of preference"[35], often allow unscrupulous merchants to win fortunes on the backs of the artists. This is something that a man like Léo Ferré couldn't tolerate, since he's an artist!

That's why recovering titles meant first and foremost reediting them immediately, in order not to see them captured again by other sharks. This is particularly evident in the world of recording and music. Seeing the waves they generate, no wonder there are so many pirate recordings, against which record publishers wanted to protect themselves from, sometimes in rather questionable ways! These include the "rigging" of CDs, to make them impossible to copy through engravers. This measure of protection is an unfair opposition to the right of reproduction, already regulated but, in fact, less and less tolerated!

* * *

Léo Ferré was therefore forced to create his exclusive and personal publishing house. Its current manager, not prepared for this job, found there, at the end of his studies, an occupation commensurate with his father's work: difficult, huge, taking up a lot of energy. His personal wishes themselves were sacrificed:

"*My dream was to go to the Caribbean and set up a fishing club, I'm really fond of fishing (...) Or the plonk: I wanted to go to Bordeaux to learn wine making, etc. My mother didn't want to hear of it. I found myself a manager after graduating.*"[36]

A manager... who is he?

A lot of work, a challenge.

I'm starting to learn something...

Good luck, Mathieu!

PART IV

"SMILE" or Ferré, a man who lives

Thirteen

The Artist and his Public

*L*ÉO Ferré is suitable for all ages. A statement that is always true, for it may seem peremptory: it was enough to see the very diverse public, of all ages, as well as of all tendencies, philosophies, and opinions, which covered the seats of all his concerts!

* * *

A political public, first of all – let us end it immediately with the most painful of all, since politics is, in my opinion, the worst thing.

Obviously, first of all, we'll think of the anarchist public. Anarchy, as a Ferré *"desperation politics"* has already been mentioned[37], we won't go back to that. On the contrary, I would like to think of the Ferré anarchy like a different thing entirely, to see the most pleasant and even the most honorable aspect of the singer's thoughts and actions.

Indeed, it's enough to know the two concerts Léo Ferré organized in Barcelona in September 1985. Why only that date? Ferré had nothing against Spain, on the contrary. I give as proof, in addition to *The Anarchists*, the song *Paris Flamenco*:

> *You didn't tell me the guitars of exile*
> *Sometimes sounded like a bugle*
> *You, my friend, the Spanish from the streets of Madrid*

Encountered last winter a flower on the lips
Let's be totally honest: Léo Ferré sang in Spain in 1985 *because Franco had already been dead for ten years*. It was his main reason. Moreover, he strove to wait ten years after the disappearance of the *Caudillo* in the hope that the partisans' passions had had time to calm down. Prudence and wisdom…!

Five years later, Ferré will take part in a show at JC Averty, entitled *Love Anarchy Léo Ferré 90*. Recorded the previous year and broadcast in 1990, this very long TV show – 2 hours 30 minutes of music and songs! – had as a main goal to (re)create before the cameras the least known works of the Ferré repertoire. Very jealous of the completeness of his catalogue, like all musical artists, Léo certainly wanted to make these songs known, traumatized that some of the choices had been decided by his former publishers - Barclay in particular.[38]

Television showed Ferré a lot in that time, between 1985-1990. For instance, a Michel Drucker show, where Léo was invited, was to be used to promote the album *You're not serious at 17*[39]. Having responded enthusiastically to the call of the celebrity presenter, Léo Ferré had to leave room for the youngsters, particularly to the distressing performances of Vanessa Paradis, then the young darling of hits-parades, who occupied the stage for an hour and a half, while Léo Ferré only sang… *two* songs!

* * *

Still, no one could blame Léo Ferré for not understanding or not loving young people. Thus, many concerts, especially during 1987, took place at the MJC. It was then that we became aware of the singer's attachment to the young audiences, at the same time as it was officially noted the growing popularity among youngsters – of which I already talked about it[40]. But let's leave Léo to explain it himself:

"Primo, I go where I find public. Secundo, because I practice rates that allow modest people to pay Ferré. Tertio, I don't have megalomaniac requirements from a technical point of view."

Oh, kindness and simplicity! Which will be rewarded with a special tribute in July 1988, when Ferré will be invited to the *Francofolies de La Rochelle*, which will have a subtitle in the form of a tribute: *Ferré's Party*.

***

For sure, Léo Ferré wasn't interested in that space. It can be seen by knowing his refusal of honors. Thus, he will decline three main ones: an invitation of honor to Victoires de la Musique in December 1988; an offer to conduct the orchestra of the Bastille Opera in July 1989 for the Bicentenary of the Revolution – Ferré doesn't want to owe anything to the state; finally, the medals and decorations that Jack Lang, then Minister of Culture, wanted to award him with…

I am Léo Ferré or I'm not!

Fourteen

A Genius of Parody

Léo Ferré's writing is a huge parody. This is an indisputable fact. It is also the main feature of his literary and even harmonic genius.

To be convinced from the beginning, it's enough to know what writing meant for him:

"I had the phrase in my hands, like a grenade before the burst. Oh well, I'll throw words into the crowd at random and books will not be used anymore (...)"[41]

Thus, with Léo, written language is a kind of permanent offensive that, *ipso facto*, is a parody of the offensive act by itself. The poet, the musician, the one who expresses himself by these means, can't do without measuring himself with the words and the audience who receives them. The poet doesn't write, he isn't content with just writing: he expresses and, to do this, parodies expression itself.

But was the twentieth century one of expression? Didn't it rather seek to censure by means of diversion, that is to say, in particular, by burying any form of expression in a uniformed mold? Much has been said about the lack of freedom of expression of the past centuries, but did the 20th century really free speech? According to Ferré, it didn't:

"We live in an epic era that started with the steam engine and ends with the disintegration of the atom (...) Should poetry feed on nuclear accumulators

and put the human soul and its disarray in an herbarium?"[42]

Wanting to transcend this era and the danger that, according to him, it represented to poetry, Ferré, as soon as he became publisher by founding the houses Owl of the Sunset then Memory of the Sea, has worked with joy and enthusiasm to create interactions between music, poetry and painting. It's especially obvious in the work *I talk to anyone*, where he links the works of painters like Charles Szymkowicz with his texts, which become themselves, thanks to the particular layout, pictorial works, so to speak. An originally successful parody!

* * *

It was from the parody and intuition he had that Léo Ferré was always aware of – and will be - being marginalized, the only response to the stereotyped poetic creation he feared. To the nuclear disintegration of his century, he responds with that of words, concepts. Thus:

When I slip into the text
The wave takes all my blood
I then sleep under a pretext
That I happily adulterate
I am the sex of the sea (...)[43]

In addition to the paronomical parody between sex and text, we'll retain from this revealing extract, the parodies of the forced birth of poetry, of expression itself, by means of a penetration of thought into the original parent element – unless it is a perpetual, spontaneous generation between the creator and the element of his creation…

The question still remains…

Fifteen

In a Madness of Colors and Sounds

IN madness, really ? Yes, and in several senses of the term!
Léo Ferré was an artist, it will never be said enough times. An artist in the true sense of the term, that is to say, in the sense that seems to me the most true – although to tell the truth, this opinion isn't only mine alone, far from it!

An artist, is above all a free person, who first creates, who can further on edit, produce, like many of them did – like Ferré[44] – and this, in all freedom, as they want, when they want. It's what Ferré always wanted to do and which he only accomplished, as we have seen, starting from 1976.

Consequently, an artist can become accustomed to creations and productions that surprise, confuse, fascinate even. This is what Ferré has constantly been committed to doing, as his love of the public was sincere. You were dedicated to your public, Léo, that was always the most beautiful, the most cordial of your intentions. You've never denied it, until the end of your life. Such fidelity can be compared to Barbara's, when, addressing her audience, she sang: *"My best love story is you..."*

* * *

Many well-meaning people allow themselves to say, when they judge an aging artist: *"He would do best to stop."* Or, Léo Ferré has always proclaimed peremptorily: *"The day I will not be heard singing anymore, I will be dead."*[45]

He kept his word.

Thus, the year 1983 was one of particularly intense Ferré production. We can first report a box of four records – beating the triptych record of the previous year! – containing *The Opera of the poor* and *The song of the owl*, recorded in just twelve hours!

Thereafter, the recitals will take place: seven in 1984, only in France, then, starting with the next year, tours in Italy, Germany, Austria, Belgium, Tunisia, Québec, Poland, in the ex-GDR... till Japan, where we find him in the summer of 1988! Everything turns, everything flies around the violins of the ball Ferré, one would say!

He doesn't forget to honor his personal opinions or of those who share them. Thus, on February 1st, 1986, he will open the Libertarian Theater of Paris or TLP, also name Déjazet Theater. This is where he'll give all his Parisian concerts till his death - the only exception: Monaco, October 21st, 1991, on the occasion of his 75 years; he thus shows what he is capable of to those who find him too old for the job!

* * *

And the records?

On my part, I remember the year 1989 well, the one where I bought my first CDs and my first stereo with appropriate drive. That year is the year of CD fury, the struggle of cassettes for their own survival and the disappearance of vinyl beauty.

For Léo, this "fury" will not be without challenges. It must be said, of course, that he himself never feared to reissue some of his titles on several different discs. Still, the various transcriptions of his vinyl recordings on CD will make it even worse: quickly, quickly, we have to reissue them! So, editing on fast-forward, with all that connotation in this phrase, the least of which is not arbitrariness and disorder! A CD offers more space than an old 33 rpm? It's perfect: we'll pass the songs on the compactor, without respecting their original release dates or even their scheduling according to the albums they once belonged to. The mane of the "old lion of the song" had thus to find many occasions to bristle with anger! Fortunately, Ferré was not a tech maniac[46], otherwise he would have been indignant at the quality of the sound of the first CDs, in fact inferior to those of the old 33 rpm...!

Léo Ferré will probably only get one satisfaction, the last one, by recording himself the last record in 1991, on which he puts to music *A season in hell* by Rimbaud. An ultimate and magnificent tribute to a gifted poet...

Sixteen

Ferré 2008

LÉO FERRÉ left us on July 14th, 1993. At the time of writing, it's been fifteen years.

Already, the year before his death, fatigue outweighed the desire for creation and representation, since the show planned at the Grand Rex in Paris couldn't take place, Ferré having to be hospitalized. Still, he'll make use of the last of his power, surrounded by his family, to develop his collection of texts *The bad seed*. It is the land of Tuscany, so dear to his heart since he lived there with Mary, who will take his last sigh.

In 2003, Léo Ferré continues to be ranked with artists who, according to the audience and even music critics, resemble him - one wonders why –: Brel, Brassens, Moustaki, Béart, also Gainsbourg... Since well before this year, he has served as a model for either protesters or whistleblowers, even international singers, like Joan Baez, or to *composers* – Léo would have liked that term – who claim him: Higelin, Lavilliers, Léotard, as well as his friend Francis Lalanne.

He had his interpreters, the old ones – Catherine Sauvage, Juliette Gréco, Édith Piaf – and the modern ones – Nana Mouskouri, Florent Pagny –, to the point that we come to consider *Jolie Môme* and *Paris Canaille* as original creations of these artists. Not to mention others, like Souchon, Cabrel or Goldman, who approached Ferré's works, but without intervening in his creations, no doubt out of respect for their creator.

There are also those who dreamed of imitating him: Alain Bashung, especially, who admits his admiration for the album *Eh Basta!* And even some rappers…!

From all of this, a constant remains: Ferré will remain Ferré, inimitable, untouchable, not a "sacred monster", a title he would probably have refused, but rather a polymorphic and polyphonic creator.

On this, I would compare Léo Ferré with the great instruments, the organs, because all the instruments, therefore all the harmonies, are encompassed in it, increasing the possibilities of expression. Léo Ferré was able to ensure, in a way, the great organs of poetry, as an expression, showing to the public that it is a polysomic whole and not a collection of ideas dear to the educators of the future toiling masses or a meeting of pretty phrases, for the least informed listeners…

A reader, present in a library where I laboriously assured a book signing a few years ago, confessed her fear of seeing poetry disappear soon.

I answered with a question:

"Do you know Léo Ferré?"

She didn't reply, no doubt for fear of appearing ignorant but went, I noted with joy, to the door of the discotheque…

She would have probably liked to meet Léo Ferré.

Oh, well! Even in our age of Internet and communication or information to excess, dare I say, she hasn't finished discovering Léo!

That's right, this is what lasts, doesn't it?

See you soon, Léo !

Always, Ferré…!

Excerpts of Fundamental Texts

Aturally, these songs come to mind, the one « made » Léo Ferré stay in the public's memory :

C'EST EXTRA
*Une rob' de cuir comme un fuseau
Qu'aurait du chien sans l'faire exprès
Et dedans comme un matelot
Un' fille qui tangue un air anglais
C'est extra
Les Moody Blues qui chant'nt la nuit
Sur un satin de blanc marié
Et dans le port de cette nuit
Un' fille qui tangue et vient mouiller...*
———
*A dress of leather like a spindle
Qu'aurait du chien sans l'faire exprès
And inside, like a sailor is
A girl who sings an English air
C'est extra
The Moody Blues singing in the night
On a white wedding like sating
And in this night's port
A girl who sways and comes to dock*

WITH TIME
With time...
With time, they go away, everything goes away
We forget the face and we forget the voice
The "heart beat stop", there's no need to go further
Searching further, let it go and that is very well

YOU'RE NEVER SERIOUS AT 17...
Poem by Arthur Rimbaud,
Titled *Novel (September 29th, 1870)*

You're never serious at 17
One great night, full of pints and lemonade,
You've had enough of cafés, so you stroll
Beneath green lime trees on the promenade...
The lime trees smell so good at night in June!
Sometimes the air's so soft it makes you blink.
The wind from off the town is charged with noise
And smells of grape, of ale and stronger drink . . .

THE RED POSTER
Poem by Louis Aragon, titled *Stanzas to remember (1955)*

You demanded neither glory nor tears
Nor organ music, nor last rites
Eleven years already, how quickly eleven years go by
You made use simply of your weapons
Death does not dazzle the eyes of partisans.
You had your pictures on the walls of our cities
Black with beard and night, hirsute, threatening
The poster, that seemed like a bloodstain,
Using your names that are hard to pronounce,
Sought to sow fear in the passers-by.

SENTIMENTAL COLLOQUE
Poem by Paul Verlaine

In the deserted park, silent and vast,
Erewhile two shadowy glimmering figures passed.

(...)
In the deserted park, silent and vast,
Two spectres conjured up the buried past.
(...)

'How sweet was hope, the sky how blue and fair!'
'The sky grew black, the hope became despair.'

Thus walked they 'mid the frozen weeds, these dead,
And Night alone o'erheard the things they said.

« *I GIVE YOU THESE VERSES...* »
Poem by Charles Baudelaire

I give you these verses so that if my name,
A vessel favored by a strong north wind,
Fortunately reaches the distant future's shore,
And some night sets the minds of men to dreaming

Bibliography

You can consult with interest the following works :

1) by Léo Ferré :
- *Phonograph testament*, edition 10/18, 2001.
- *Benoît Misère*, edition The memory of the sea, 2001
- *Poet… your papers!* edition Folio/Gallimard, 1977
- *The Bad Seed*, edition of Livre de Poche, 2000

2) on Léo Ferré :
- CUESTA, Stan. *Léo Ferré,* edition Librio, 2002.
- FRIGARA, Claude. *Léo Ferré, entretiens entre peau et jactance (1983-1991),* Christian Pirot editor, 2003.
- Collectif. *Cahier d'études Léo Ferré n°1* "La marge", edition of Petit Véhicule, 1999.
- Collectif. *Cahier d'études Léo Ferré n°2* "Words…Words…Words", edition of Petit Véhicule, 1999.
- Collectif. *Cahier d'études Léo Ferré n°3* "De toutes les couleurs", edition of Petit Véhicule, 2000.
- Collectif. *Cahier d'études Léo Ferré n°4* "Écoute-moi", edition of Petit Véhicule, 2000.
- Collectif. *Cahier d'études Léo Ferré n°5* "Muss es sein – Es muss sein", edition of Petit Véhicule, 2001.
- Collectif. *Cahier d'études Léo Ferré n°6* "Technique de l'exil", edition of Petit Véhicule, 2002.

- Collectif. *Cahier d'études Léo Ferré n°7* "Marseille", edition of Petit Véhicule, 2003.

3) Works of poets who particularly inspired Léo Ferré:
- APOLLINAIRE, Guillaume. *Alcools.* Gallimard, 1987. (Coll. Poésie).
- ARAGON, Louis. *Le Crève-cœur. Le nouveau Crève-cœur.* Gallimard, 1980. (Coll. Poésie).
- ARAGON, Louis. *Les Poètes.* Gallimard, 1976. (Coll. Poésie).
- ARAGON, Louis. *Le Roman inachevé.* Gallimard, 1980. (Coll. Poésie).
- BAUDELAIRE, Charles. *Les Fleurs du Mal,* Le Livre de Poche, 1977.
- VERLAINE, Paul. *Fêtes galantes. Romances sans paroles* preceeded by *Poèmes saturniens.* Gallimard, 1973. (Coll. Poésie). Éd. J. Borel.

Favorite Discography

I Really want to do for this special page what biographers never do, at least those who are content to only tell the story of a life: to propose an anthology among what I like best of Léo Ferré.

I see all the arbitrariness, but I don't regret it: everyone is free, of course – me too. With this small book, I wanted to share my passion for Ferré, communicate my analysis of him.

Others have done it, so I also did it.

For the rest, you'll see!

* * *

I am a poet, I admit to this sin. I particularly liked:
- *Verlaine et Rimbaud*, album Barclay published in 1964: 14 poems of Verlaine (*"Écoutez la chanson bien douce..."*) and ten from Rimbaud (*"Je m'en allais les poings dans mes poches crevées..."*)
- *Baudelaire*, album Barclay published in 1967, with editing by Jean-Michel Defaye. From *Spleen* to *Vert Paradis*, reliving the *Fleurs du Mal*, not as your teachers presented them to you, hoping to make you pass the exam with knowledge as it was conceived by the Mammoth, but let them sing in your hearts: with the National Education and its measures with which it always tried to bend the poets, it was damned in advance, I grant you. With Ferré, everything is possible...
- *Léo Ferré chante Aragon*, album Barclay published in 1961. Like everyone else, I let myself be rocked by *The red poster, This is how

men live and *I sing to pass the time*. But it's totally ok to love others as well...
- *You're never serious at 17*, album EPM[47] published in 1987 (with the photo of Mathieu Ferré on the cover and another, with his father, in the small notebook inside the CD). It's especially poetic, since Léo sings Rimbaud (the title track), Verlaine *(Sentimental Colloque)*, Baudelaire *(I give you these verses)*, Apollinaire *(Marie*, a song whose title he had to choose rightly!), as well as songs of his own, mostly from his collection *Poet... your papers!*[48] *(The dead who live, The just sleep, The fake poet...)*

And I'm a Ferré fan, with a strong preference for compilations. So I also enjoyed:
- *Léo Ferré – The Golden Disk*, album Barclay published in 2000. A compilation which gathers 12 of Léo 's best titles: *The Poets, Thank You Satan, This is how men live, They voted, C'est extra, Memory and the sea, With time*, etc.
- *Léo Ferré (l'Été 68)*, album Barclay published in 1969. His best disc, by excellence, or so they say! On my part, I totally agree *(See Chapter 9 on this subject).*
- v *Les indispensables de Léo Ferré*, a compilation published in 1988 by Sony Music Media. It includes the titles of Léo's youth: from *The time of the Tango* to *Plastic Time*, moving on to *The Guinche, The Poor Man's Piano, Paris canaille, Anarchist Seed, Poor Rutebeuf, The Room, The Seine*, etc.
- v *Je te donne*, album CBS published in 1976, recorded in Italy with the Orchestra from Milan directed by Léo Ferré himself. Among the 7 titles that it contains : *I give you, Death of the Wolves, Love, The Coriolan Overture* (Beethoven), *The Superlative, Requiem*, I especially love the song *Muss es sein – Es muss sein*, wink from Ferré to Beethoven.

Now, it's for you to choose!

Interesting Websites

~~~ ⚘ ~~~

ost websites given below are both biographical and commercial. I would have liked more artistic ones! Nevertheless, it's ok to take up this task, for those who have the time!

1. an abandoned site, sadly: www.leo-ferre.com.
2. the very lively site of the association *Thank You Ferré* : www.leo-ferre.org.
3. a fan website: perso.club-internet.fr/rigaudin.

Notes

WHO ARE YOU, FERRÉ?

1   The Violence and the Boredom in phonograph Testament, p. 57.
2   Y en a marre in The bad Seed, p. 104-105.

THE BEGINNING OF A CHILD OF THE ENTERTAINMENT

3   Beethoven, very much in love with liberty, wanted to dedicate this symphony to Napoleon as soon as he entered German territory, because he represented the continuation of the Revolution. Then, learning that the Emperor of the French was building personal power, he renounced to this dedication.
4   He nevertheless graduated from Political-Sciences in 1939.

A COMPOSER BEFORE ANYTHING ELSE

5   Léo Ferré will only marry Marie (Marie-Christine Alfonso) on the 5th of Mars 1974.
6   See Chapter IX.
7   This is actually the preface to the collection *Poet... your papers!* read with musical accompaniment.

THE POET, THE POETS

8   See previous chapter.
9   *The Poets* in *The bad Seed*, p.96.
10   See Chapter XV.
11   *Heartbreak* (see Bibliography).
12   In *Ferré sings Baudelaire* (op.cit.).
13   I bring testimony by experience.

THE SINGER, THE SINGERS

14 Quoted in epigraph by Stan Cuesta in *Léo Ferré* (Librio).
15 See Chapter VIII, XIV XV.
16 This album will know in 1977 an Italian version: *La musica mi prende come l'amore*.
17 See on this subject the article of Stéphane Oron in the *Léo Ferré Workbook n° 5* « Muss es sein ? Es muss sein ! », p. 9 (see Bibliography).
18 See Chapter X.

WITH TIME...

19 See Chapter IV.
20 ... which was briefly replaced by the "double cassette" then, and nowadays, by the "double CD's", but always in the same spirit!
21 In *Cahiers d'études Léo Ferré n°4* "Listen to me", page 60.
22 *Op. cit.*

LOVE-ANARCHY

23 Texte publié sous ce titre dans le recueil *la mauvaise Graine*.
24 See Chapter I.
25 Pronounced [zou].
26 *Love anarchy Ferré 70*, or Léo poses with the *Moody Blues*.
27 *You're never serious at 17* (1987).
28 See Chapter XI.

THE PRODUCER

29 In truth, it's the orchestra from RAI (Italian television).
30 See Chapter IV.
31 I, myself, only discovered it by writing this biography!

LÉO-BENOÎT, FERRÉ-MISÈRE

32 See on this subject the article of Jacques Layani in *Study notebooks on Léo Ferré n°6* « Exile Technique », pages 136-137 (cf. Bibliography).
33 *Ibid.* (page 138).

MEMORY AND THE SEA

34 Let's remember *Difficult times* (3 different versions in the album *The artist's life* (reissue CD Barclay 1999).
35 A leonine clause by which a publisher forces an author to automatically give him all his future titles, without the publisher being obliged to publish them. Any

honest publisher must contribute to the disappearance of this abuse, and any author who is reasonable and concerned with his rights will be obliged to be wary.

36 Quoted by Stan Cuesta in the work *Léo Ferré* (see Bibliography).

THE ARTIST AND HIS PUBLIC

37 See Chapter IX.
38 See Chapter IV.
39 See favorite discography.
40 See Chapter I.

A GENIUS OF PARODY

41 *Style*, in *The bad Seed* (page 145).
42 *Preface* in *Poet... your papers!*
43 *Memory and the Sea* in *The bad Seed* (p. 132).

IN A MADNESS OF COLORS AND SOUNDS

44 See Chapter X.
45 From an interview given to *Matin de Paris*, on October 28th, 1983.
46 See Chapter XIII.

FAVORITE DISCOGRAPHY

47 This acronym stands for a new record company run by François Dacla. EPM officially means: *Marketing Production Edition*. But a tenacious legend wants Léo Ferré to translate this acronym as *Et Alors Merde…! And then, shit... !*
48 See Bibliography.

About the Author

Born in Remiremont (France) in 1960, Thierry Rollet has devoted himself to literature since the age of 15. Associate to Gens de Lettres de France. He published his first book at age 21 and is now at his 38th published book. First a teacher, he founded in 1999 the Scribo company, which handles the distribution of books, literary advice to authors wanting to be published, training in French / English and a writing workshop. Thierry Rollet has published novels, collections of short stories, historical accounts, and many novels in magazines and on the Internet.

You can connect with me on:
- http://www.dedicaces.ca
- https://twitter.com/Dedicaces
- https://www.facebook.com/Dedicaces